BRAND YOURSELF ROYALLY
IN 8 SIMPLE STEPS

BRAND YOURSELF ROYALLY
IN 8 SIMPLE STEPS

Harness the secrets of kings and queens
for a personal brand that rules

Nancy Blanton

EDB

Ellys-Daughtrey Books
Fernandina Beach, Florida

BRAND YOURSELF ROYALLY
IN 8 SIMPLE STEPS

Published by Ellys-Daughtrey Books
P.O. Box 15699, Fernandina Beach, FL 32035

ISBN: 978-0-9967281-0-2

Printed in the United States of America
CreateSpace version

Cover image: Her royal highness sitting on a throne.
© NejroN Photo. Bigstockphoto.com

For Jane, Sue, Ray, Dave, Vicki,

Tom, Marlys and Andrea,

and as always, for Karl

MORE BOOKS BY
NANCY BLANTON

Sharavogue: Winner of Florida's Royal Palm Literary Award. A novel of 17th century Ireland. A peasant girl vows to destroy Oliver Cromwell on his bloody march to crush a rebellion, and then she must run for her life. Can she survive plantation life in the lawless West Indies to return, confront her sworn enemy and reclaim her lost heritage? Available on Amazon.com, iBooks and barnesandnoble.com.

Heaven on the Half Shell: The Story of the Northwest's Love Affair with the Oyster. Includes recipes from historical cookbooks. Winner of the Council for the Advancement of Science in Education (CASE) award. Available on Amazon.com and online booksellers.

The Curious Adventure of Roodle Jones. For ages 3 and up, the story of a day's romp with Labrador Retriever Roodle Jones and her friends, with a happy conclusion. Illustrated by the author. DogSez Press, CreateSpace edition. Available on amazon.com.

For publication updates, subscribe to the author's blog at
www.nancyblanton.com

ACKNOWLEDGEMENTS

Over the course of a career, one learns from many different individuals and circumstances, and may not even realize at the time what she or he is learning. For some unknown reason, while in graduate school I chose corporate advertising as my primary focus of study, and that is where my education on branding began. It has been a magnificent jigsaw puzzle ever since, but it is coming together nicely.

First, foremost and with undying gratitude, I must thank my friend, former boss and long-time mentor Jane Kilburn. From her I learned how to handle countless situations. She saw something in me I could not see myself, and gave me opportunities that built not only my confidence, but also the passion for my work. If it's a jigsaw puzzle, she gave me all the edges.

In addition to Jane I have learned from many others. Sometimes, even when they may have thought they were learning from me, I was still learning from them. In the interest of brevity I thank the following individuals (in random order) for their time with me, the professionalism they showed me, and the creativity and love for communications, marketing and graphics they shared with me:

Sue Nixon and Ray Ueno, Ardent-Sage; Dave Miller, Stoke Strategy; Tom Clauson, Total Creative; Vicki Loe; Sandra Noel; Yvonne San Luis; Marilyn Farrell; Lorraine Howell; Elaine Long; Marlys St. Laurent; Melanie Skaggs; Laura Smith; Mayo Ochiltree; Rob Walgren, Chris Nardine; Andrea Patten; Chuck Barrett; Terri Dean; Eddie MacEoin.

And not the least is my darling husband Karl Shaffer, (aka Mr. Wonderful) whose gift is the time, opportunity, support and encouragement to write my heart out. And I must add that I have contributed to his life, too. He now knows what an em dash is and how to make it—a shared experience we'll never forget.

CONTENTS

Introduction: A Royal Undertaking...................................1

A Royal Legacy 5

A Royal Persona...9

Good Queen Bess...13

The Sun King...19

Personal Glory...23

Honest Abe to Camelot..27

Eight Simple Steps...33

Step 1: Values 39

Step 2: Core Brand Driver 43

Steps 3 & 4: Vision & Mission 47

Step 5: Positioning...51

Step 6: Taglines...55

Step 7: Marks 59

Step 8: Colors 63

Putting It To Work 67

All About Trust 75

Author Bio 77

Image Credits 78

Selected Sources 81

INTRODUCTION:
A ROYAL UNDERTAKING

As an author of historical fiction who has a strong background in corporate branding, I've often considered the brands created by history's icons. For centuries, kings and queens had to create their personal brands for some of the same reasons corporations use branding today—mainly to be memorable and likable by their audiences, and to differentiate themselves from their predecessors or perhaps pretenders to their thrones.

Think of Henry VIII, for example. He was not exactly the icon of honesty, charity and good will, was he? But in his day, most of the people of England would never meet him, and yet would be called upon to pay taxes and fees, and perhaps support an army going to war. He needed to project an image of strength, divine empowerment, wise leadership and benevolence. His public image, the persona the masses were allowed to know, provided exactly that.

I call that personal branding, even though he was the figurehead of a powerful government much like a corporation. His persona was built around a single person whose actions could make or break the success of the brand.

The basic process of branding remains much the same

between corporate and personal branding. A strong identity is created to represent the business or individual, and to suggest the value in products or activities of that entity. If the entity makes the commitment to that value and consistently delivers it, trust will develop among customers. Over time, the symbol of the brand, or logo, can by itself trigger a feeling of trust. And trust, in turn, generates more business. But there are significant differences between corporate and personal branding also, especially for an author, artist or consultant.

Corporations typically generate many products and may have whole families of brands that fall under one overarching brand, like Microsoft or Kraft. Managers of these brands struggle to create a personal connection with customers in hopes of building brand loyalty, but often fail because of the general mistrust of corporations. That's why you see them posting in social media, trying to humanize their organization.

While an author or individual may be generating multiple products for sale similar to a corporation, the individual is always selling his or her self. Using the author as an example, if readers try and like one of your books, they will look for anything published in your name to continue reading your voice, your style and your command of storytelling. It's the consistency of quality that will keep them coming back because they trust that you will deliver. The difference with an author or individual is that customers begin to feel that they know you. They're attracted to the values and personality that show through your writing. Like Henry, you can't go around meeting every customer and talking to them about your values, right? So personal branding can help you communicate who you are more broadly and efficiently.

Branding doesn't mean you need to design your own

personal logo. Brands are about much more than logos. The most successful brands focus on creating the most positive experience a customer may have, from product to personality to customer service and more. A brand does involve imagery, but it is based on some very serious soul searching and groundwork. Once that is done, the rest falls into place more easily, the imagery makes sense, and you don't have to reinvent it every time you need an ad, a poster or a one-sheet. That's where the efficiency comes in.

But first, who are you? And what is your brand?

Many who talk about branding say it's a concise and compelling statement about what you do and how your products are better than any others. And that's one way of doing it. But the strongest and most enduring brands in the world go deeper. Their brands are based on values. Instead of telling customers what you do (they already know that), tell them *why* you do it. What drives you? What gets you up in the morning? What is that belief deep in your core that stokes your passion and makes you work so hard? You must find it, and it must be authentic. Write that statement, and from that will flow all the elements of your personal brand—what the eight steps in this book are all about.

It bears repeating, your brand must be authentic. I can't imagine an author successfully projecting a persona that is not real because the truth will show up in your work. If social media had been around in King Henry's time, no number of portraits, statues or proclamations would have protected his brand against the tweets, Instagrams and blog posts that would have exposed his true self.

But that's another story...

In the first six chapters of this book, we'll learn from several royals who were masters at defining and communicating their brands. At the end of each chapter, you'll find "Gems from the crown," or bits of wisdom you can adopt for your personal branding.

Then we'll apply those Gems as we work through the last seven chapters including the eight simple steps to complete your personal brand worksheet.

At the end the steps you'll find a bonus feature: I'll walk you through the process of writing your own communications plan to put your brand into action.

As the title of this book says, the steps are simple, and they are. But that doesn't mean they're easy. As you start, be willing to invest some time and thought into each part of the process. You may be thinking about things you hadn't considered before, and along the way you might learn something about yourself. The time you spend on your personal brand is valuable and will serve you for years to come.

When you turn the page to begin, remember this: you are your flagship, you are your storefront, you are your corporate headquarters, and you are the king or queen. And throughout the process, you may be a tyrant. You answer only to yourself.

In this, it is truly all about you!

1

A ROYAL LEGACY

In the introduction, I talked about the differences between corporate and personal branding, and how values rather than product should be the core driver for the brand. Because kings and queens were probably the first successful users of personal branding, we can learn from their practices.

In ancient Egypt, if the monuments and pyramids attest, rulers valued nothing more than a legacy. Not only to be remembered by their people but also to help open the doors to a prosperous afterlife.

Way back in 1479 BC, Hatshepsut became the sixth pharaoh of Egypt's 18th dynasty, one of few women to achieve that post, and she ruled successfully for more than 20 years. So concerned about legacy was this queen, she had an obelisk at Karnak inscribed, "Now my heart turns this way and that, as I think what the people will say—those who shall see my monuments in years to come, and who shall speak of what I have done."

When her pharaoh husband died, she became regent to serve while her infant stepson came of age. Hatshepsut saw a unique opportunity and took full advantage of it. She had herself declared king. But now, especially because she was a woman in a man's role, she had to take steps to secure her throne.

In the media of the day—stone carvings—she portrayed herself as a man complete with false beard, Khat head cloth and shendyt kilt, muscular shoulders and small breasts. (In fact, archaeologists have discovered she was obese, had very large breasts and suffered from a skin disease, the salve for which probably contained toxic chemicals that may have led to her death.)

She also renamed herself "Maatkare," a combination of words meaning truth, soul and Sun God (Re), suggesting she was in direct contact with the god and thereby legitimately held her throne.

In pursuit of her legacy, she focused on two things: architecture and art. She built roadways and sanctuaries, erected commemorative obelisks, and carved her immense temple into the limestone cliffs near Thebes, containing more than 100 of her statues in various religious poses. Hatshepsut was everywhere. Even though her stepson did everything he could to erase her legacy from history, most of it still remains.

Gems from the crown

And so, what four things can be learned from Hatshepsut's strategies for establishing a personal brand?

First, a defined set of *values*. For Hatshepsut, they were leadership and legacy.

Second, *opportunity*. You may not be able to declare yourself king, but you can identify a niche where you may reign supreme, that has subject areas that speak to you (like Re) and stir your passions enough to keep you interested. That's important because branding is a long-term relationship.

Third, *focus*. Hatshepsut didn't try to do everything but focused specifically on a few main things that addressed her values. She promoted trade, which made it easier to obtain the things she needed, like building materials for monuments, and art from all over the world. You may have many demands on your time and resources, and you still need time to create your products. Don't participate in every charity, try to attend every event or be on every social media platform. *Focus* on the ones that really serve you and fit who you are.

Fourth, *endurance*. A strong brand will endure. Note that Hatshepsut's has been around for nearly 3,500 years. Most of us can remember corporate brands we grew up with as kids, even if the companies that created them no longer exist. I'll bet you can think of some brands right now that still play their jingles in your head. Some authors have amazingly durable personal brands, their names alone conjuring mental pictures. Hemingway? Melville? Austen? Dickens? Twain? And the list goes on and on...

2

A ROYAL PERSONA

If England's King Henry VIII had been an author, who might he have been? Authors, like royalty, can project certain images to create a persona in the minds of their audiences and the general public, to thereby be remembered and gain policy support, or book sales as the case may be. King Henry was able to create and project a persona that met his needs, and the author that comes to mind for me is Ernest Hemingway.

As young men, both Henry and Ernest were good-looking with athletic physiques. Henry was known for having "an extremely fine calf to his leg," for example. Both played hard at sports, be it jousting or hunting, and both projected that masculine imagery and larger-than-life persona that continued long after the men themselves were gone.

King Henry's brand persona

Henry VIII valued education, religion, architecture, arts, innovation and ostentation. He used his physical size to advantage—he was 6'2″ at a time when most men were considerably shorter—and in many cases his portraits show him taking up most of the canvas. In the background of some portraits, he was surrounded by the cultural sophistication reminiscent of imperial Rome.

He excelled at sports and held jousting matches wearing his gilded armor, satin and pearls to show his wealth, strength and power to visiting dignitaries.

To promote his campaign for church reformation, he had pamphlets created and broadly distributed, and paid theatrical and minstrel groups to travel the land and to portray Catholic priests as devils while he was the defender of the true faith. (I once led a branding road show for employees in various departments, but in our case the devil was the chaotic past and the new brand was the hero.)

In architecture, the exterior of buildings included hundreds of busts, the laurel-wreathed heads of emperors and military heroes, suggesting they were the foundation upon which the Tudor dynasty was built.

In art he was featured at the center of huge architectural structures in classical style, in at least one case receiving the water of life and the book of life directly from the angels—a clear reference to his religious persona as head of the Church of England with the divine right of kings.

Later in life, even after a jousting injury and other health conditions changed him dramatically—and even though the noble king was responsible for about 70,000 executions—the persona he created still resonated. Fans of the *Tudors* television series may recall the last episode just before Henry dies. He orders the portrait artist Holbein to change his latest, and accurate, depiction of declining, sickly Henry into the standing image of the strong, virile (note codpiece), magnificent king he wanted his people to see.

In part, Henry's brand persona enjoyed long-term success because the powerful, charming, man's man image he created was something the citizens of his time wanted and respected in their king. Such an image was easy for them to accept and easy to follow because it met with their own personal values. Even in the face of horrible truths it was difficult to let go.

Gems from the crown

What wisdom does Henry offer?

First: *Define yourself clearly.* Use your own values and interests to demonstrate the person you are to your specific audiences, as Henry used sports and architecture.

Second: *Align your persona* with those things that are also important to your audiences. Which of your values will resonate most with your customers? What are they looking for that you can offer? Demonstrate through your persona that you're the person who can be trusted to deliver.

3

GOOD QUEEN BESS

Sometimes called Good Queen Bess, Gloriana or The Virgin Queen, the second daughter of Henry VIII became Queen Elizabeth I of England at the age of 25. She quickly and masterfully defined herself in the eyes of her people—that is, she established her personal brand.

At a disadvantage from the beginning because she was female, Protestant and the daughter of the executed Anne Boleyn, she also was coming into power after the death of her half-sister Mary, called "Bloody Mary."

Elizabeth needed to establish a firm base of power that her courtiers and her people could respect and accept. In her case, facing the likelihood of Catholic assassins, a strong personal brand truly was a matter of life or death.

Values and positioning

Elizabeth had been in training for royalty for a long time. She knew what she wanted: increased world trade, supreme naval power, religious unity and economic prosperity. She didn't care for war but did not shrink from it if her power or her nation were at risk. To those ends, Elizabeth not only created a powerful persona but also "positioned" herself as a strong and just ruler, a noble and formidable king in a gentle woman's body.

Positioning defines you to your audience in a positive and memorable way while differentiating you from your competitors or predecessors.

If I were to quickly write Queen Elizabeth's positioning statement, first I would beg forgiveness for being so bold and admit a royal positioning statement would require a lot more serious thought and development time. That said, it might go something like this:

For the people of England, France and Ireland, we (the royal we) descend under divine right from Britain's greatest monarchs, to establish peace, religious unity, international trade and naval dominance, and to maintain their well-being, security and prosperity.

- Elizabeth first based her claim to the throne on history, descending from the Trojans, linking to King Arthur and Henry VIII. This history provides the background for her many symbolic portraits, and to this she added color choices, iconography, and especially consistency.

- Elizabeth didn't care to sit for portraits so eventually artists were given "approved" facial forms to paint from, adding to the consistency and agelessness of her persona.
- She preferred white gowns to emphasize her fair skin and bright hair, and augment her image of purity. Her courtiers had their own portraits painted wearing Elizabeth's colors—black, white, red and gold. (Red and black dyes were costly to obtain and process, so garments in these colors signified wealth.)

Power of portraits

Elizabeth had no media to broadcast her message, so she filled her portraits with imagery to establish her persona. After the defeat of the Spanish Armada in 1588, the famous portrait on page 13 shows her with her feet upon a map of the world, her hand upon the globe and her fingers across the Americas. In the background, Spanish ships are driven to dark destruction while English ships enjoy the sunlight.

"Elizabeth's savvy in regard to managing and manip-ulating public opinion was substantial. She spent lavishly on gowns, jewels, portraits and royal prog-resses, whistle-stop horseback tours of her domain that let her see and be seen. Her skill with rhetoric, both visual and verbal, was undisputed, as in the legendary speech delivered to her troops on the eve of the Spanish Armada. The queen, dressed in an Athena-like white gown and silver breastplate, told her men, 'I have the

body of a weak, feeble woman, but the heart and
stomach of a king—and of a King of England too."
~ Hanne Blank, Virgin, The Untouched History

In what is known as "the pelican portrait" she wears pearls indicating purity, the Tudor rose for unity, and a pendant showing a pelican mother caring for her young. In Elizabeth's time, mother pelicans were icons for self-sacrifice and symbolized Elizabeth as mother and protector of her Protestant nation and her subjects.

Like a virgin
Elizabeth became famous for her virginity even though many believed she'd had a long-term love affair with the Earl of Leicester. She was celebrated as the Virgin Queen in portraits, pageants and literature.

In younger days, Elizabeth's virginity represented purity, innocence and chastity, making her a perfect bride for some wealthy prince. As she aged, her virginity symbolized the sacrifice of herself (her chance for love and family) for her country, lending an air of holiness to her reign.

Wings to fly
Immortalized by the poet Edmund Spenser in his epic *The Faerie Queen*, Elizabeth was represented as a goddess, the embodiment of beauty and virtue. In reality, about this time

her skin had been damaged by smallpox, she'd lost much of her hair and had to wear wigs and heavy makeup. Still, her gowns in some portraits are magnificent constructions of high shoulders and great wings. The Rainbow Portrait was painted when Elizabeth was in her 60s, but the gown is one of her sexiest, with white floral bodice and an elaborate head-dress, a mantle over one shoulder, a cloak with eyes and ears motif, the serpent of wisdom on her sleeve, and in her hand a rainbow with the motto "no rainbow without the sun." She reminds me of the recording artist Cher in this one: ageless and outlandish.

In spite of many difficulties during her reign, Elizabeth remained popular and was praised as the ruler of a golden age. Following her death in 1603, the date of her accession was a national holiday for 200 years.

Gems from the crown

What can be gleaned from Elizabeth's positioning in terms of personal branding?

First, your persona must support your positioning statement.

Second, once developed your positioning can guide marketing strategy and tactics to serve you for the long-term.

Third, the choices you make to represent your brand, such as colors, imagery and messaging, should be thoughtful, consistent and repeated.

4

THE SUN KING

It should come as no surprise that when it comes to personal branding, the French take it to a higher level. The Sun King, Louis XIV, is the most outstanding in a long line of Louis who had impressive nicknames: Louis the Young, Louis the Lion, Louis the Saint. These guys had the right idea of the personal brand. And then, there were a few who kind of botched it: Louis the Quarreler, and Louis the Prudent, the Cunning, the Universal Spider.

But the Sun King has transcended the centuries,

reigning longer than any other monarch of a major European country (more than 72 years, 1643-1715). He is memorable for centralizing government, for his lavish Palace of Versailles, for his grand poses (and shapely legs), and of course for his fashion sense.

Taking back control of his country from the Catholic cardinals, Louis XIV valued fiscal and military reform, law and order, the arts, and thriving French industries that could be taxed. To move forward with his goals, he had to start by eliminating the mammoth corruption and embezzlement by some of his advisors.

He gained the respect of the populace by focusing first on law and order, and relied on his new government ministers reporting directly to him to help establish and maintain his public image. King Louis understood that the display of magnificence and splendor created part of a king's power. He also knew the value of repetition. His portraits were numerous, and his images were distributed far and wide to reach as many of his subjects as possible. According to Peter Burke, author of *The Fabrication of Louis XIV*, "Louis saw himself everywhere, even on the ceiling." His personal symbol, or logo, was the sun, and anything that bore his standard—his bed and his dinner table even if he was not present—was to be respected as if he himself were there.

Brand guidelines

To maintain a consistency of image and message in all of this repetition, there had to be rules, and Louis understood this as well. In all its forms, his public representation had to convince the audience of his greatness. Louis identified with admired historical figures such as Clovis, the first Christian king of France, and Charlemagne. So, the artists, musicians and writers drew from such powerful images as a Roman triumph, an equestrian statue with the horse stomping some evil. In state portraits he was:

- Larger than life, his eyes higher than the viewer
- Dressed in armor symbolizing valor, or clothing showing his high status (elaborate wigs to enlarge the king's impressive stature)
- Surrounded by powerful props such as globes, scepters, the sword of justice, thunderbolts and laurels
- Wearing the expression and posture of dignity and grandeur

"As for the expression on the royal visage, it tends to vary between ardent courage and dignified affability. A smile is apparently considered inappropriate for the King of France," Burke wrote. In addition to portraits, sermons, sonnets, poems, literature, plays, coins and tapestries all had to present the king in this idealized light.

Brand strategy

To help implement his brand, King Louis had Jean-Baptiste Colbert who devised and documented a strategy whereby the king would be glorified as a patron of the arts. This "communications plan" included a list of all the various media where the king could not only invest but be depicted, as well as a list of individuals, their strengths and weaknesses, who could be called upon for the work. This is akin to the modern-day communications plan that incorporates the guidelines, employs the strategies, sets specific goals and messages, and chooses the right media partners to reach target audiences most effectively. (More about this in Chapter 15.)

Like the sun, King Louis rose with the work of his reign and the help of his brand advisors, but in later years experienced a "royal sunset" when expensive wars, fragmented politics and a shortage of talent contributed to the decline of his popularity. There would be two more Louis to rule France before the French Revolution of 1789, but none to reach so high a zenith.

Gems from the crown

What can we learn from the personal brand of the Sun King?

Again, that values rather than fashion must be the brand driver (but fashion does have its place).

Guidelines are necessary to maintain the brand's consistency and its power.

A well-considered and written strategy helps ensure the brand is made visible and relevant to its target audiences.

5

PERSONAL GLORY

For using personal branding to advantage, Napoleon
Bonaparte was truly the emperor among history's royals.
In Getty Museum's book, *Symbols of Power in Art*,
Napoleon gets his own chapter, "A Case Apart." Historian
Jules Tulard wrote, "There have been more works written
about Napoleon Bonaparte than there have been days
since his death."

His mother said Napoleon behaved like a ruler even
from an early age (sounds like a typical toddler to me)

but struggled to fit in at school. He spent a lot of time alone reading, thinking and dreaming. At age 16 he wrote, "Always alone in the midst of people, I return home in order to give myself up with unspeakable melancholy to my dreams. How do I regard life today?"

His dreams even then must have been powerful for, while he valued revolution and political reform, what he wanted most was personal glory. His path was through military leadership and successes, and once he advised one of his generals to concentrate on "strength, activity, and a firm resolve to die with glory. These are the three great principles of military art which have always turned fortune favourable to me in all my operations. Death is nothing; but to live defeated and without glory is to die every day."

Tulard regarded Napoleon's brand persona as "the myth of the savior," truly the great leader on the white horse, bringing power, prestige and glory to France. Napoleon had a brilliant understanding for how to maintain this image using portraits, objects and writings.

"From carefully falsified army bulletins, to paintings and engravings, to the jewelled snuffboxes adorned with his portrait and distributed to the bishops who officiated at his coronation as Emperor, Napoleon knew how to create a cult of personality that maximised his popularity and sought to win the loyalty of those who might oppose him."
~ **Gemma Betros**, *History Today*, "Napoleon the Man"

His portraits are carefully constructed to show him as a fierce and valiant military leader on the white horse, a

thoughtful and compassionate government adminis-
trator, a god-like ruler with the scepter of Charles V and
the hand of justice of Charlemagne. Eagles on carpets
and furniture symbolize
imperial power, bees embroid-
ered into clothing symbolize
industry. His feet do not touch
the ground but rest on ornate
pillows, indicating his godlike
authority. In these images he
invested heavily, but he could
not tolerate criticism and
worked to suppress images
that opposed this persona.

*"When he rose to power in
1799, Napoleon Bonaparte had serious concerns about
comedic references to his personage. He immediately
ordered the closure of all satirical papers in Paris and
let it be known that cartoonists who toyed with his
image would be dealt with severely. In 1802, he tried to
insert a clause into the Treaty of Amiens with England
stipulating that any British cartoonists or caricaturists
who used his image in their art should be treated in the
manner of murderers and forgers. The English
rejected the unusual amendment."*
~ Nichole Force, blog post on the dangers of humor

Over time, Napoleon's ability to suppress negative
information was unsuccessful, especially when military
defeats and other issues began to fray his persona and
reveal the divergence between the image and the man.
Portraits depict his rise as a young officer and his

dramatic decline brought on, according to some historians, by his swollen ego and perhaps the remnants of the lonely teenager he had once been.

"Where the eager young officer would energetically mine others for advice, and the self-assured First Consul could openly admit to being wrong, as Emperor Napoleon became increasingly reluctant to hear the opinions of advisors, gradually preferring to work long hours in a solitude that suggested not so much ambition as quiet desperation as he led France to defeat."
~ Betros

Gems from the crown

The wisdom from Napoleon includes caution.

A personal brand persona must *align with the actions* of the person. You've heard the old saying, actions speak louder than words. When what you exhibit or say differs from what you actually do, you break down the trust that is essential to any brand, personal or corporate.

Prepare your brand for *transparency* rather than duplicity. Misrepresentation is almost impossible to maintain and, in the long run, will get you smeared.

Always be willing to *listen to trusted advisors* and well-intended feedback. Just as every writer needs an editor, every person needs to understand how he or she is seen from the outside. Most people want you to succeed, and their advice won't always be helpful, but it is worth listening to just in case. It can help to temper those things that drive you, so they don't drive you into the ground.

6

HONEST ABE TO CAMELOT

"Character is like a tree and reputation like a shadow.
The shadow is what we think of it;
the tree is the real thing."

~ Abraham Lincoln

American presidents are not royalty, coming to power via
election rather than bloodline, but they still enjoy many
of the protocols of European royalty covered so far.
Presidents have used personal branding as a primary
weapon in their get-elected arsenal. Several American

presidents have had outstanding personas, but two are particularly remarkable: Abraham Lincoln and John F. Kennedy. Their brands are so strong that you almost automatically think "Honest Abe" and "Camelot."

Every school kid knows the story of the impoverished Abraham Lincoln, growing up in a log cabin and reading books by candlelight. As Alan Brew writes, "Lincoln's life exemplifies what has been variously labeled 'the American dream,' or 'the right to rise' from rags to riches. In Lincoln's case it is quite literally a rise from a log cabin to the White House. His story is the embodiment of the Lincoln brand: gritty determination, honesty, family values, unswerving belief in America and the basic rights of his fellow men. His life offers a powerful testimony to dream. It is what ordinary Americans want to believe about social mobility and the opportunity to get ahead."

In fact, Lincoln was a highly intelligent lawyer and one of the first presidents who was actively branded and marketed to the voting public by his political campaign. Sociology professor and author Jackie Hogan said in an interview, "There were all kinds of theatrics: pulling up a fence rail and parading around saying this fence rail was split by Abraham Lincoln. They created an image of him as an average Joe, and in many ways, he was not an average Joe. But he was very happy to ride that reputation into the White House."

What Lincoln had that other presidents—and royals —lacked, was access to new technology, and he used it to advantage to receive and distribute information. This new technology was the telegraph. Used primarily by the banking and financial industry, Lincoln was the first president to use it for wartime communication.

"The telegraph increased the speed at which information and communication could be received. It changed the world, it changed war, and it changed daily life."
~ Scott Scanlon

Lincoln certainly had his detractors. It would be impossible not to, leading a nation in the time of a civil war, but he rose to power through his intellectual leadership, and in many cases was able to diffuse contentious situations through his powerful oratory. He was able to define, in elegant and often poetic layman's terms, the sides and meanings of an issue.

Today we might call that "content marketing." Like presidents, authors and consultants have a lot of information at their fingertips. Mining that information and either sharing it or providing analysis that is useful to an audience helps you acquire and retain customers.

Though some thought Lincoln's physical appearance awkward, he did try to look the part in support of his brand. The black frock coat made for him by Brooks Brothers included a hand-stitched eagle in the lining with the inscription, 'One Country, One Destiny.' This was the coat he was wearing when he was assassinated.

Lincoln came to the presidency when the nation was deeply divided. By contrast, John F. Kennedy took office on a wave of prosperity, the post-war boom. And where Lincoln had use of the telegraph, Kennedy had television:

"Once a commodity that few Americans with money possessed in the late 1940's, it was now in the homes of all Americans by the era of the 1960's. It was this medium that would blast across the screen the youthful,

*handsome, rich John F. Kennedy with his young
beautiful wife Jackie and their two vivacious children."*
~ xroads.virginia.edu

In the 1950s and 60s, when families were watching *Ozzie and Harriet* and *Father Knows Best* on TV, the Kennedy family exemplified that perfect, happy image, and Kennedy allowed his family and particularly his children to be photographed "under his desk, in their playrooms, in the Rose Garden, in their schoolhouses, throwing parties, Caroline riding her pony, or John-John running toward the helicopters and planes which so often captivated him."

Kennedy also used his charisma for rallying people around an aspirational cause that they already wanted, such as being first on the moon, or creating the Peace Corps. And, it helped him to conceal his private side. Certain issues (including his serious medical issues, extramarital affairs, connections to organized crime, and a plot to assassinate Fidel Castro) were not to be revealed by the media, and remained secret until investigative reporters of the 1970s got into the files.

Gems from the crown

From United States presidents, the following advice:

First, it pays to *know your audience* and what they want. Both Lincoln and Kennedy understood their times and identified their personas with the ideals of the time. Even though they were faced with difficult issues and circumstances, their personas helped them maintain public support through crises, and have survived the decades. Both Lincoln and Kennedy were assassinated in office, and one might argue that this propelled them into indelible memory. That may be true, but their powerful personas live on.

Second, it pays to *use technology to advantage*. Today's social media offer unprecedented access to audiences where they live and within their particular areas of interest. Consistent messaging and a strong brand story can create a memorable personal brand that will stand for you when you need it most.

Third, just as you create your own persona, *create meaningful content*. Think about your target audience and what they need from you, clarify how to reach them best and provide useful information that aligns with your values. It is not as hard as it may seem. You probably already have the right content, it just needs repackaging.

7

EIGHT SIMPLE STEPS

*"The secret of getting ahead is getting started.
The secret of getting started is breaking your complex
overwhelming tasks into small manageable tasks,
and starting on the first one."*

~ Mark Twain

What can authors and truly anyone who needs a personal brand really use from the royalty discussed in the previous chapters? First and foremost, remember that we are all the kings and queens of our own brand. I once heard a story about Sir Paul McCartney's road crew complaining of how difficult he was to work for because of his controlling and demanding management style. McCartney's response? Hey, it's *my* name on the marquee at every show, not yours. In other words, it's your brand, and also your job to protect it.

A quick review of the royal gems we've collected so far provides a good reference for the branding steps you are about to begin:

Definition. Values are the basis of your brand and help guide what you will and won't do in your business and in your life. In personal branding, communicate things that reflect those values. Customers want to engage with real people who have values they can respect and admire.

Opportunity. You can't be all things to all people. Find a niche that will allow you to shine.

Focus. Choose subjects or activities that address your values. Don't participate in every event, charity or social media option, just those that really serve you.

Endurance. A strong, consistent brand can endure. Note that Hatshepsut's brand imagery has been around for nearly 3,500 years, Lincoln's for 150 years.

Persona. To be memorable, project and highlight real personality features that will resonate in the minds of your audiences.

Positioning. Your positioning statement should distinguish you firmly in the minds of your audience relative to others in your field, and guide your marketing strategy and tactics for the long-term.

Alignment. Make sure your persona aligns with your positioning statement and vice versa, so that what you do consistently reflects your brand values. Consistency builds trust and trust attracts customers.

Colors, imagery and messaging. Use these to support your positioning and persona. Be consistent, and repeat them wherever your brand appears.

In writing. Written guidelines help to maintain the brand's consistency and therefore its power. A good written strategy helps ensure the brand reaches its target audiences and helps keep you on track.

Listen. Always be open to the well-meant input of trusted advisors.

Use technology. What system provides the most direct route from you to your audience, and how can you use it best? And remember, content is king! Make sure what you are offering is useful to your audience.

Know your kingdom

In any kind of communications activity, the first thing you need to know is who you are talking to, and what they need. Who is your audience? Depending on your work and the types of writing you do, you may have one audience or several.

- Are they distinct or do they overlap?
- What do they need from you?
- How do they get their information?
- What do they expect from you as a professional and as a communicator?

Think of one or two, or maybe a handful of individuals from your primary audience. What are they like? As an example, I write historical fiction and my stories tend toward the hero's journey and social milieu, and not so much toward battles and blood (although those are not completely absent). My readers are male and female but a higher percentage female. They love to read, love history and strong female characters. They want to be immersed in time and place, but also learn while they read. They are busy, smart and social.

I must always have this target audience in mind when thinking about my brand, and it helps me decide how best to express it, where and when. You can go into much greater detail than this, and define subgroups as needed if you write in more than one and very different genres.

How can you learn about your audience? If you are a member of a writers' association or professional guild of some kind, you may have access to market studies providing a wealth of information. You can also

- Watch comments in social media
- Read reviews of others in your genre or category

- Talk to them in stores or at events
- Ask friends

And relax. It is not a perfect science no matter what the professional marketers say. In my case, I learned that some historical fiction readers were tired of the Tudor period and the proliferation of books on that era when so many other periods in history are not well covered. Also, I knew many readers are hesitant to invest in an 800-page novel. Who has time? I had heard complaints about authors who overplay their research and include every detail instead of just what is important to move the story forward.

So, I targeted those readers by setting my story in a different time period, making sure it was fast-paced, under 300 pages, and selective in detail. The result was successful and effective, but now some of my readers tell me they love the story but maybe it moves too fast and they don't want it to end. They want it longer. They love learning about a period in time they have not read about before but normally would not have looked for it when shopping for a book.

Perhaps I created a higher barrier to overcome in that readers aren't familiar with the period I've chosen or why they might want to read about it. But that's okay, it is an exciting era, and highlighting this has become my challenge and my mission: to illuminate, entertain, inform and inspire my readers.

Your personal branding worksheet

Over the next eight chapters, I will walk you through each step of a personal branding worksheet, and how to put it into action. First, take a look at the Eight Steps listed below. These are the elements of your brand. Ultimately you will write sentences or paragraphs after each item to complete the entire list on a single page.

As you work through each chapter you will be thinking about yourself and your work, answering questions, making lists, writing and rewriting statements. You may be scribbling on notebook pages. I suggest you create your own e-document and list these elements, leaving space between each one where you can fill in the content you're about to create. Once you've arrived at the statements you like for your brand, you can add them to your worksheet.

VALUES

CORE BRAND DRIVER

VISION

MISSION

POSITIONING

TAGLINE

MARKS

COLOR PALETTE

Let's get started!

8

STEP I: VALUES

*"We believe people with passion can change the world
for the better...and that those people who are crazy
enough to think they can change the world,
are the ones who actually do."*

~ Steve Jobs, Apple

Your brand is not really about what you do. It's about
why you do it. Steve Jobs said Apple's brand was not
about a company that makes computers. It's about a
company that values innovation, passion, aspiration and
simplicity. Apple's products support people who have
those same values.

You write books? That's great—a lot of people write
books. Your readers are interested in *why* you write
them, what makes you tell the stories you tell. When I am
at a speaking engagement, people don't ask much about
my book. They ask where I get my inspiration, what is my
writing process like, and why did I make the choices I
made about time, place and characters. The answers go
back to who I am and what I believe in. The values that
are most important to you are the building blocks of
your brand.

There are so many values, a good way to start
narrowing them down is to pick from a list.

VALUE WORDS

Approachability	Faith	Perceptiveness
Artfulness	Fascination	Perfection
Assertiveness	Fearlessness	Perseverance
Audacity	Finesse	Persuasiveness
Benevolence	Flexibility	Philanthropy
Brilliance	Focus	Playfulness
Charity	Fortitude	Polish
Clarity	Fun	Precision
Cleverness	Gallantry	Professionalism
Commitment	Generosity	Reliability
Compassion	Grace	Resilience
Confidence	Gratefulness	Resolve
Connection	Heroism	Resourcefulness
Consistency	Honesty	Respect
Conviction	Honor	Rigor
Conviviality	Humility	Sagacity
Coolness	Humor	Self-reliance
Courage	Imagination	Sensitivity
Creativity	Impartiality	Shrewdness
Credibility	Independence	Simplicity
Curiosity	Industry	Sincerity
Daring	Ingenuity	Sophistication
Decisiveness	Inquisitiveness	Solidarity
Determination	Inspiration	Speed
Devotion	Integrity	Spirit
Dignity	Intelligence	Spirituality
Directness	Intensity	Spontaneity
Discipline	Intrepidness	Stability
Discovery	Intuitiveness	Strength
Drive	Inventiveness	Synergy
Duty	Judiciousness	Thoroughness
Dynamism	Leadership	Trustworthiness
Effectiveness	Liveliness	Truth
Elegance	Longevity	Valor
Endurance	Love	Victory
Enlightenment	Loyalty	Vigor
Energy	Mastery	Virtue
Entertainment	Meticulousness	Vision
Enthusiasm	Mindfulness	Vitality
Excellence	Motivation	Vivacity
Exhilaration	Openness	Warmth
Expertise	Originality	Wealth
Exploration	Outrageousness	Wisdom
Expressiveness	Passion	Wonder
Fairness	Peacefulness	Zeal

Some companies ask their customers to select from a list the values they believe describe or reflect the company, and then the company uses those words in their brand materials. Or, they may take the opposite approach, choosing different words to help highlight specific values they want their audiences to recognize. Either approach can be effective as long as it's done with honesty.

> *"Great ambition is the passion of a great character. Those endowed with it may perform very good or bad acts. All depends on the principles which direct them."*
>
> *— Napoléon Bonaparte*

On the previous page, I've provided a list of more than 100 values. You can use this list or find larger lists if you type "values list" into your search engine.

Look through and choose values that are most important to you. Use the note pages at the end of this book to make a quick list, then narrow it down to 10 or 20 words you think define you as a person and as an author, artist or consultant. Be honest. As we learned from Napoleon, it doesn't pay to pretend to be something you are not, and it will be difficult to maintain a false façade.

With your short list, narrow it down again to five or six values that define you but also are important to your audience. These are areas where you may be able to connect with them on a personal level. Values like leadership and generosity might be areas where your audience can relate to you. Hygiene and poise are good values, but these may not be things you'd use to define your brand and, unless they are the topics of your books they may not rise to the top level of your brand values.

Once you have your values defined, it's wise to sit with them for a day or two to make sure you like your choices and feel confident they capture exactly what you want to project to your target audience.

Do you like your final list? If so, add the values to your worksheet. If not, try going through the process again with a trusted friend. Sometimes it's difficult to think about your own values, but an objective friend can see them immediately.

When you have them captured, you are ready to take on Step 2, your core brand driver.

9

STEP 2: CORE BRAND DRIVER

"You must tell a story worth telling
to be a brand worth sharing."

~ Simon Mainwaring

What is a core brand driver, exactly? It is what gets you out of bed in the morning and what keeps you going throughout the day. For Hatshepsut, for example, it was her drive to build a lasting legacy. For Napoleon, it was personal glory.

It's that perpetual torch of passion about what you do, stated in a concise and easy-to-remember way so that you and your associates can buy into it and live it. Why do you need this? Because it's your divine right to rule, your staff of royal power.

You need a "brand driver" for external and internal use;
the short phrase that captures the essence of your idea.
For example, take GE: "imagination at work." This is
important so employees know how to make decisions
that align with the brand. FedEx is great example…
what's their promise to customers and to themselves?
On-time delivery by 10:30 am. If you ever watched [the
movie] Castaway, *remember the way that brand*
promise unified everything for everyone in the early
scenes? And that last scene where he delivered the

package: that's delivering on the brand promise.
~ Allen Adamson, Brand Simple

A core brand driver is not a tagline, although it may sound like one and look like one, and your tagline may be derived from it. And you may think, "Hey, what I do is difficult and complex, and can't be captured in a simple phrase." That's probably true, and reducing all that complexity to its essence is no easy task. But think of it as a rallying point, a war cry. It may also be your unique selling proposition. What is the one thing about your work that, if you didn't do it, the world could not become a better place?

Derrick Daye of *Branding Strategy Insider* wrote that brand essence is usually expressed as "adjective, adjective, noun." Here are examples that may be helpful:

Disney: Fun family entertainment
Nike: Authentic athletic performance
Starbucks: Rewarding everyday moments

Notice Disney says nothing about movies or theme parks, Nike never mentions shoes and Starbucks has nothing to do with coffee. It is about the *essence* of what you do, not the product. You can state your brand driver the way these companies have done it, or in any number of ways, but I like it stated as a challenge.

To come up with my own, I boiled down my feelings about my work to one personal belief, that we are all part of a continuum of the spirit. What is accomplished in one generation affects other generations both before and after. My storytelling satisfies an unfulfilled need from long ago and has the power to change perspectives even just a little bit. I am an author of historical fiction. My core brand driver is:

Illuminate the past to inspire the present.

Or, using Daye's format:

Informative inspirational storytelling

The best way to create your phrase is to objectively examine what drives you. It may be one thing or several. Brainstorm with intention. Write down everything that comes to you and see what rises to the top.

Don't allow yourself to worry about what other people might think. Remember, your brand driver is not for the public, it is for you. List the best options, read them, say them, feel them, and gradually you'll find the right combination of words and hear the choir *sing*.

10

STEPS 3 & 4: VISION AND MISSION

*"Your vision will become clear only when you
look into your heart. Who looks outside, dreams.
Who looks inside awakens."*

~ Carl Jung

Now, doesn't it make you happy to have your core brand
driver in place? It is like discovering your purpose in life.
Step 3 is about thinking through your brand driver to
the best possible conclusion. What would the world look
like if you are wildly successful? For me, the world would
be a literate place where everyone would learn from
history and wouldn't repeat the mistakes of the past, so
things like human brutality, greed-driven wars and
preventable famines would no longer exist.

Remember the movie *Jerry Maguire*, with Tom
Cruise and Renee Zellweger? Jerry stays up all night in a
hotel room, inspired and passionate about his work, and
writes a manifesto. He shares it at his office, then loses
his job for it because others don't want to go along. But
that manifesto drives the way he operates his own
business and ultimately leads to his personal success.
The beauty of a personal brand is that you need not
worry about others going along. You are the creator, the
grand exalted ruler, and executor of your vision.

Let your imagination go on this one. Try to capture

your perfect world in a sentence or two. But it is *your* vision, so if it takes a paragraph or a page, just let the words flow. Maybe you have never really thought this through before, but now is the time and the process is important. This is really about why your newfound purpose in life matters, *and it does.*

Write it all down with as much clarity as you can muster. Then add it to your branding worksheet. Refer to it when trying to make an important business decision about whether or not to do something. Will this something help you realize your vision, or does it divert you from that path?

STEP 4: MISSION

Creating your vision is a major accomplishment. You have defined your universe! Now, let's bring it down to boots on the ground. Your mission statement is about what you do every day in service of your brand driver and toward achieving your new world vision. A good mission statement should be:

- **Specific**. Leave the blue-sky language for your vision and driver. The mission statement should be as clear as possible for your external audiences.
- **Focused**. Capture in broad terms what you do and how that adds value to the world and the experience of your customers and audiences.
- **Memorable**. Keep it brief and easy to remember. When someone asks you what your business mission is, you'll know it. They'll be impressed, and maybe they'll remember it, too.
- **Motivating**. A "mission" is something special you are supposed to do. Let it inspire you every day.

- **Personal**. Your mission statement should reflect your persona, your brand personality as discussed in Chapter 2 (remember King Henry VIII?).
- **Lasting**. Your mission statement is partly definitive, partly aspirational. Preferably it will stand the test of time, but don't worry about getting it perfect. Just commit to something you are comfortable with based on what you have worked on so far, and be willing to make changes if your world changes. Many businesses tweak their mission statement regularly to reflect current business conditions.

In the 2014 annual report, the CEO of General Electric presented the company mission with this statement, followed by the explanatory paragraph:

GE'S MISSION IS TO INVENT THE NEXT INDUSTRIAL ERA, TO BUILD, MOVE, POWER AND CURE THE WORLD.
GE imagines things others don't, builds things others can't and delivers outcomes that make the world work better. GE brings together the physical and digital worlds in ways no other company can. In its labs and factories and on the ground with customers, GE is inventing the next industrial era to move, power, build and cure the world.

Note how this mission statement provides a broad umbrella to capture everything GE does without being cumbersome. See how it might inspire both employees and customers? Your aspirations may not be quite so lofty, but your mission statement can allude to your vision and what you will do to achieve it. Note GE's reference to labs, factories and customer contact as specific ways the company will accomplish the mission.

Still need inspiration? Do an online search for nonprofit mission statements. These are most likely to correspond to author, artist or consultant needs. Then search for some corporate statements for comparison. Pay particular attention to the strong and aspirational words they use.

Keep in mind your mission statement is something you may want to post on your website, so think about it from the reader perspective. Does it communicate what you want them to know? Consider getting feedback from friends or colleagues to make sure they understand it the way you intend it. Go for clarity over cleverness. Mission statements are not easy to write, but the good news is you are still in charge and have all the votes!

11

STEP 5: POSITIONING

"Ye may have a greater prince, but ye shall never have a more loving prince."

~ Elizabeth I

To develop your positioning statement, I refer you back to Chapter 3 on Queen Elizabeth. Because of political pressures, Elizabeth's life was at stake so it is understandable that she needed strong positioning in the minds of her subjects. But why do *you* need a positioning statement?

If you are an author, just go to a bookstore like Barnes and Noble and look around. Most likely, you will quickly be overwhelmed with the vast number of books and wonder why you even bother writing at all. Get out of there fast and remember your brand driver and your mission. You are one of a kind. No one else has the same story and no one else can tell it the way you do. But how can you stand out in the marketplace, and how will you explain it quickly to the potential customer standing next to you in an elevator?

To create a good positioning statement you should (1) define your target audience, (2) include the category or genre in which you operate, (3) articulate the benefit or unique qualities being offered and (4) give customers a reason to believe you will deliver on your promise.

You've already done most of the footwork on this one.

What we're doing now is packaging it in a way that brings in your marketing strategy and how you want your audience/customers to perceive your brand in relation to all the others. The trick, in this case, is to get emotional. How do you want your customer to *feel* when they think of you? To get the answer, you really have to step into the skin of the customer and ask, "What's in it for me?"

We are all self-centered consumers in that we want to know we are getting value for our money and our time. A "good product" is important, of course, but it isn't enough to gain your foothold in a highly competitive world. A good product that makes me feel X, or a good product that gets me Y, is what can distinguish you above your competitors. What makes you special or different in a way that can touch customers on an emotional level? You will probably find the answers in your vision or core brand driver. Knowing your audience and what they want is essential. Consumer decisions are based on emotions.

"Researchers have shown over and over again that emotions are not only an important part of decision-making, but are critical to the process. In fact, one neuroscientist, Antonio Damasio, did research showing that brain-injured patients who had experienced damage to the part of the brain where emotion is generated could no longer make decisions."
~ Gail Kent, The Buzz Factoree

A popular blog post from Cornell University (See "How to Write Market Positioning Statements" by Doug Stayman at blog.ecornell.com) gives you all you need to write a good positioning statement, including guidelines, a simplified template, examples, and even a free "statement generator."

To start, try this fill-in-the-blank template:

For [insert Target Market], the [insert Brand] is the [insert Point of Differentiation] among all [insert Frame of Reference] because [insert Reason to Believe].

Here's my attempt using the template that you might use as an example:

For readers of historical fiction, Nancy Blanton is the award-winning author of Irish history adventure novels, combining research skills with a passion for Irish heritage to both inform and entertain.

This statement distinguishes me from other authors of similar books, and suggests to the reader they are in for some good storytelling. It also suggests the things I need to hit on in my blogging and marketing programs.

Your positioning statement will guide your marketing and can help you create your tagline, but it is not a tagline and generally is not intended for public view. What's the difference between the two?

The following page shows examples that demonstrate how the positioning statement is for the business while the tagline is for the consumer.

Positioning statements:
- Target: Style on a budget.
- Volvo: For upscale American families, Volvo is the family automobile that offers maximum safety.
- Home Depot: The hardware department store for do-it-yourselfers.

Taglines:
- Target: Expect more. Pay less.
- Volvo: For life.
- Home Depot: You can do it. We can help.

Take your time, be creative, and allow for flexibility so you can update it when the needs of your audience change.

12

STEP 6: TAGLINES

"Imagination governs the world."

~ Napoléon Bonaparte

Starting with this chapter, we move into the last three steps of your brand, focusing less on what is behind the curtain and more on what your audience actually will see. These three elements—taglines, marks and colors—are much easier to develop once you've completed the earlier sections that give a full understanding of your audience, your brand basis and core driver, your vision and mission. Your positioning statement helps clarify exactly what your audience needs to know.

These elements also call into play a basic rule of communication, and particularly electronic communication—the three-second rule. You've heard of this rule with regard to food dropped on the floor (is it still safe to eat?) and most likely in basketball (a lane violation), but it also applies to websites, advertising and any visual communication—like book covers. The rule is, you have three seconds to capture a person's attention. Either it is visually compelling to hook your readers, or they bounce off to another site, pick up another book, turn the page, goodbye.

Many things are constantly competing for a person's

attention these days. If you can't grab them fast you've lost them. That's why good headlines and strong graphic design are critical to your brand. Your tagline may be the only thing someone reads, so if it hooks the reader it has done its job. The big thing to remember is the lesson from Napoleon Bonaparte, who eventually lost the trust of his supporters. Make sure your tagline represents you faithfully and promises only what you can deliver.

Creating a Tagline

Everyone does not need a tagline. Primarily they are intended for advertising, but businesses do use them as a hook on websites and signage and in numerous other ways. The essential thing is to use it consistently and *do not waver*. Wherever you use it, make sure the words, capitalization and punctuation are exactly the same. Make sure it is clearly readable. And make sure it is unique and appropriate (which means you'll need to do some searches to confirm that your brilliant idea has not already been used and trademarked by someone else.)

Many people think writing a tagline is easy, and there certainly have been some classic tags that resulted from a sudden lightning bolt of brilliance. But most of the time a good tagline requires creative thought about all the brand elements, focused brainstorming, and trial and error.

"A great tag line is memorable, enlightens people about your business, and differentiates your company and product from competitors. Generally, a good tag line is a short, catchy phrase with an interesting and positive message delivered in 3-6 words."
— simplewebsiteservice.com

Taglines can highlight your brand and your unique selling proposition in a number of ways. There are five styles of taglines:

- Strong claim
- Showcase benefits
- Showcase company
- Question audience
- Reveal customer emotions

For an author, consultant or any personal brand, you are showcasing yourself and your values, so the third option may be the best choice, but I would not rule any of them out. Brainstorming should not be constrained.

Start by looking at the websites of other authors or professionals you admire:

- What is your first impression?
- Do they use a tagline? How is it used?
- What words do they use to describe themselves?

Think about those words, borrow those you like, and list others you can think of that describe what you do.

Next, think about your audience and try to answer this question: Why should they be interested in you and what you do? Answer in as many ways as you can. Consider your particular strengths, your style or approach. And think about what makes you different from others in your category. You have already thought about these things to develop your positioning statement, but now you must settle even deeper into the consumer mind.

Put the consumer on the royal throne for a few minutes, and yourself on bended knee before them. You have a few seconds of the monarch's most precious time. How might you appeal to them, and perhaps entertain a bit, to engage them in a most positive way?

For me, I considered my passion for Irish history, and decision to write it as an adventure with selective detail and a faster pace compared to others in my genre. I wrote my tagline as a call to action:

Embark on an adventure in Irish history.

It may not be the world's best tagline, but I think it would raise the monarch's eyebrow, and that's enough to get me to the next sentence. Already this tagline has been effective in hooking attendees at book festivals.

Do some brainstorming by yourself or with someone else who knows you well. When you have a few options you like, test them on some friends or readers via email, Facebook or in person. See which option resonates most, and then make it work for you everywhere: your website, business cards, postcards, posters, one-sheet and wherever else it makes sense for you.

13

STEP 7: MARKS

*"I strive for two things in design: simplicity and clarity.
Great design is born of those two things."*

~ Lindon Leader

A "mark" is a general term for that single graphic that stands for you, and would represent you when you cannot be physically present. It won't work in the same way as King Louis XIV's standard—no one would be expected to bow when they see it, for instance. But a well-made mark or logo *reminds* people of you and what they get from you, generates good feelings and can lead to sales.

For an author, artist or consultant, in most cases your mark would be your name, and you might choose a particular typeface to use consistently. You may be tempted to choose some of the more graphic typefaces, like Edwardian Script for historical fiction, Thriller for thrillers or mysteries, or something a little wild like Mistral or Giddyup to get attention. Resist temptation! You will be far better served choosing something that is clean, professional looking and always appropriate.

If you work with a graphic design professional (highly recommended), your designer can help you find a typeface that could work well on book covers and repeated in all of your promotional materials. Once you've selected a typeface, stick with it even if you are bored and tempted to try something new. Your signature typeface becomes a core part of your visual brand.

Independent authors and business owners may need an identity—a logo—that can be used for book imprints, advertising, business cards and other promotional materials. In this case, the best way to start is by doing some research. Who do you admire in your field? Who are your competitors? Do some online searches to see what typefaces, colors and graphics they use. Do a comparative analysis. What seems to work best? What is most compelling? How might your mark stand out in the same categories while maintaining your distinct brand persona and positioning?

Again, a professional graphic designer knows how to look at these things and can help ensure everything developed for your brand is strong, consistent and competitively viable. They also can make the process fun, rather than scary or tedious. If you choose to design your own, there are a few things to remember:

- **Always keep your audience in mind.** It is easy to get caught up in something you think looks cool, but you may be too close to the process. The graphic you like may not resonate or even make sense to your audience. I once knew a woman so enamored with a logo she'd designed she had it tattooed on her shoulder, but many who saw it could not determine what it was or what it meant. As with the tagline, be open to feedback.

- **Keep it simple**. A simple, clean design will be strong enough to hold up equally well whether you use it on the side of a city bus or the size of your pinky nail on a book spine. Don't get too detailed with fine lines and shades that might break up through various reproduction processes. Design first in black on white. Once that works you can consider colors (next chapter). Print it in various sizes to see how well it reproduces. Print media (newspapers or magazines) are typically in a deadline rush in which the quality of your mark is not their first priority. While well meaning, they can make a mess of even the best logos. A strong and simple mark will help ensure consistency and protect your brand.

- **Understand the technical side.** As we learned from presidents Lincoln and Kennedy, you want to use technology to advantage, not get bogged down by it. You will need multiple file types (such as jpg, eps, tiff) and multiple sizes to send to the various places you'll use this logo, so understand what these are and how each is used. For a website that explains this very well, look for "What Should You Get From Your Logo Designer" at thedesigncubicle.com.

And for inspiration, look no further than your Internet browser and the search term "logo for personal branding." Have fun!

14

STEP 8: COLORS

*"Color does not add a pleasant quality to design
– it reinforces it."*

~ Pierre Bonnard

Signature colors are a great way to express your brand.
Brand colors should be chosen for specific reasons. For
example, Queen Elizabeth chose white and gold to represent her purity, and red and black to express her
wealth. Courtiers who wanted to identify with her went
to great expense to wear the same colors.

In my last job, my organization operated an airport, a
seaport, public marinas and public parks. So, the brand
colors selected were light blue (air), green (land) and
dark blue (sea) and were displayed in three wave-shaped
bars indicating forward movement.

For myself I chose two shades of green, to reflect
both the color most often associated with Irish and the
prominent color on the cover of my first novel. I added a
third color of ocean blue for variety and balance. I wear
the greens at every book festival, signing or speaking
event, not as a uniform but via a scarf or a nice silk
blouse so the message is not shouted but still effective.
And, used prominently in my book displays the colors
create a strong, cohesive and appealing first impression.

You can't depend on color alone to influence your
customers' behavior because people tend to react to

colors based on their own experiences. It *can* play a role when it reflects the core values of the brand, as in Apple's use of white to communicate simplicity and their clean, uncluttered design.

The feelings, mood and image your brand creates will work together to influence your customers. The trick is to select colors that are both appealing to the majority of them but also match your brand's desired personality. There are some gender differences that might be helpful depending on your audience. The majority of men say blue is their favorite color while women are more divided between blue, purple and green. Men are drawn to strong colors while women generally prefer softer colors.

"Certain colors do broadly align with specific traits (e.g., brown with ruggedness, purple with sophistication, and red with excitement). But nearly every academic study on colors and branding will tell you that it's far more important for your brand's colors to support the personality you want to portray instead of trying to align with stereotypical color associations."
~ Gregory Ciotti, The Psychology of Color in Marketing

What colors should you choose? Here again I strongly advise working with a graphic designer who has experience with various media and how colors behave in each. Print colors do not look the same as screen colors. In one logo I worked on with a design agency, we had to choose different shades for digital screens and printed materials to ensure the greatest consistency to the consumer's eye. Professional designers can select the best options to give you greatest consistency across all media.

Think about your values, vision, mission and positioning. What colors come to mind for you? What values do you want to represent most? Is there a color that dominates your work in some way? You can browse through a color chart to get some ideas, but you will see it quickly becomes overwhelming. Each color has many shades. Which is the best one, and why?

The historic color wheel can be helpful in choosing combinations of colors:

"The colour wheel allows us to see at a glance which colours are complementary (opposite each other on the wheel), analogous (adjacent to each other on the wheel), triadic (three colours positioned at 120 degrees on the wheel from each other) and so on. Each of these relationships can produce pleasing colour combinations."
~ creativebloq.com

There are plenty of websites that can help you understand how the color wheel works and there is software available that can create a color scheme for you (see Adobe's Kuler). And of course, there are a few tricks. For example, your designer may ask for any photos, paintings or other materials that have something to do with your work. Designers call these things "assets" and will draw color choices from them. Another option is to visit a hardware store and look in the paint section. There are usually booklets and paint chip sheets that offer interesting color combinations. Find one you like and then search for the corresponding ink and web colors.

There is no definitive answer here, you will have to rely on your experience, your brand personality, your good taste and your gut reaction. It wouldn't hurt to get some friend or audience reactions, too. Whatever colors you choose, make sure you love them. You will be looking at them and working with them for a long time as your brand grows and prospers.

15

PUTTING IT TO WORK

"A brand is not a product or a promise or a feeling. It's the sum of all the experiences you have with a company."

~ Amir Kassaei

Congratulations! You have worked your way through all the steps to create your personal brand. It took only eight steps–simple, but not easy. The brand you've built will reign over your products, marketing and communications to help you build awareness and trust with your audiences. I hope you feel like royalty.

You can fill in all the spaces on your brand worksheet now so it becomes a quick reference guide for you. Over time, you may add more details and pages. Every time you create something new, like an ad, a poster, a mailer, a rack card, etc., it's an opportunity capture and save the specifications to further define your brand consistency. In this way, you also create efficiencies for yourself, because each time you need something new you don't have to start from scratch. You will already have a style and guidelines to work from.

Next Steps

Like Good King Louis, you will need a well-written plan to ensure your brand is made visible and relevant to your target audiences. Depending on your audience and products, you may decide you need a full marketing plan. These can be very simple or hugely complex, and cover all the details about price, product, placement and promotion. The contents of a marketing plan are well covered in a number of books. For a personal brand, you may need only a portion of the overall marketing plan: the Communications Plan. This plan is all about reaching your audience on a personal level.

Having written communications plans for most of my career, I have seen those that fit on a single page, and those that filled binders too heavy to lift with one hand. Here I offer you a simplified but professional option to help you launch your new brand with ease. The elements of a good communications plan include:

- Overview and Purpose
- Goals
- Audience(s)
- Key Messages
- Strategies
- Objectives
- Vehicles
- Tasks/Schedule
- Measurement
- Evaluation

Ready? We'll take them one by one.

Overview and Purpose

Okay, why bother writing an overview and purpose? This is your personal brand and you already know your purpose, right? But you may use this plan as a template for future plans. Write a brief summary of your brand and a general statement about what you hope to achieve with the plan, such as "inform readers/customers about my new brand/website/logo," or whatever you like. Be sure to date it, too.

Goals

A goal is an overarching statement, and objectives are specific, achievable action steps toward each goal. I usually list my objectives *after* I have defined the strategies because the strategies influence how I write them.

Communication goals are different from marketing goals. In marketing, the focus is on the 4Ps mentioned above, and often on increasing unit sales or expanding distribution. In communications, the goals are to increase awareness, increase understanding, change attitudes, influence behavior or drive brand messaging.

This section should list between one and three things you aim to accomplish with your communications plan. At least one of them should be numerical, such as, "I will reach ___ percent of (defined audience) with key messages about my new brand." The number will help you measure your success after the plan has been implemented.

Audience

You may have a general "audience," or it may be segmented into groups depending on how you distribute your products, how your audiences receive information, and how you interact with them. For example, one audience might be women between the ages of 45 and 70. That's fairly broad. You might define an audience as "4,053 kayakers in the Pacific Northwest." Or, it might be "Subscribers to my newsletter." See where we are going here? Be clear and specific about defining your audience, so you can be specific about how you will reach them.

Key Messages

These are messages derived from your positioning statement that you will use in all of your communications for the plan. Depending upon the complexity, you may have just one overarching message, or you may choose to break it down into two or three. I recommend keeping messages to three, and no more than five if you must. Too many messages make everything less memorable. A key message might be something like,

- (Your name) is working to create (something related to your vision) for a better future.
- Readers can learn more about (vision, good thing you do, product benefit) at (your name + event or activity).
- (Your name)'s experience in (your background, research, positioning reason to believe) drives the success of (consulting agency, new book, etc.)

Play around with this a bit and you will come up with good useful messages. Sometimes it helps to select one person from your target audience and think about two or three things you would tell this person if you met them on the street. That's right, you should try to keep the messages short and engaging.

Strategies

How will you approach the plan to make it most effective? What do you think are the best ways to reach your audiences? Can you economize by doing two things together? Is there a way you might use timing to give your audience a one-two punch of information? Will you go heaviest on printed products, email or social media? What will be your most effective mix of the options? Will you incorporate events? This is the time to think broadly about your approach, but it also helps you contain your communications to what you believe will be strongest, rather than trying to do everything. You need just a few short statements here that will be your guidelines. Specifics will come next.

Objectives

To write these, look back at what you wrote for your goals, and list them again here. Then under each, write two or three bullet points for how you will address them strategically. Be specific. For example, if your goal was to reach 90 percent of your blog subscribers, an objective might be "Publish blog content on two Thursdays in May containing key message #1, and on two Fridays in June containing key message #2." Admittedly, objectives are hard to think about and to write, but they make you work a little harder than you might otherwise, and increase your likelihood of success.

Vehicles

This is the term used for every mode you will use to communicate your messages. The list could include your local daily newspaper or radio station, TV talk show, Facebook, Twitter, blog, newsletter, poster, handouts, giveaways, etc. Anything you can use to convey a message is considered a vehicle. List all you can access that are appropriate for and open to your messages. The list helps you think through all of your options, pinpoints overlap and economies, and shows you the breadth of the audiences you will reach.

Tasks/Schedule

This is about what needs to be done, when, and by whom if it isn't you. This is where you can strategize the timing of things. For example, your blog insights may tell you which days get the most readers. Schedule postings for those days. Which days on Facebook are the best? What are the deadlines for the newspapers or newsletters? Sometimes it helps to make a table that includes the vehicle name, deadline or publication date, what kind of content you will use, and contact information if needed. Have a start and end date for the overall plan.

Measurement

After the end date, look back at your original goals. Did you meet them? Exceed them? Come close? Use whatever analytics you have at your disposal (Google Analytics for your web page, blog insights, Facebook reach, likes and comments, number of email responses, number of event participants, etc.) to create an estimate of how many people you reached in your target audience.

In addition, think of qualitative measures like verbal and written feedback. Were there any compliments? Criticisms? What other indications do you have as the result of your work? List them all to create the best overall picture.

Evaluation

This is something to write during and/or after the

execution of your plan. First, think about each product and activity. What worked really well? What didn't? What "gems" did you discover and what would you do differently next time? These can be paragraphs, just phrases, or bullet points.

Next, take an objective look at your measurements. What kind of analysis can you generate from this information? Was the strategy effective? Did you meet your goals? Were they the right goals? Was it the right audience? Can you think of a way to measure your work that you hadn't thought of before that might give you a more useful picture?

Capture it all for your own reference. Every communications plan is a work in progress; most of them get altered somehow during execution. And, there are always things that don't work out the way you thought they would. It's all great information for making your next communications effort even better.

Writing a communications plan can be tedious work, but it's also an opportunity to be creative about how you promote yourself. My best advice is to sit down and type it out in an hour. Then walk away and allow time for ideas to surface. Come back to it later with fresh eyes to refine and finish. Once it's done you'll feel a sense of accomplishment and power. You have a *plan*. And it's likely most of your competitors don't. That gives you a golden royal advantage.

16

ALL ABOUT TRUST

"A lot of brands, you can't touch them. When you're dealing with Snoop Dogg, he brings you closer to the brand and it feels like it's a part of you."

~ Snoop Dogg

The crowning glory for a personal brand, or any brand, is trust. When you are consistent with your values and offer something of value to your customers, they learn they can trust you to meet their expectations. And once that trust is established you become a part of their lives in a way, so that when they see you or see a representation of you, they have a positive feeling or response.

The job of the brand is to reach beyond where you can physically go, extending into the spheres of people you may not know but who can potentially become your customers. That's why it is so critical to maintain and protect your brand and ensure its consistency. Consistency is the key to its power.

And *you can do it*. Always remember, you are royalty—the absolute ruler of your own personal brand.

Well done, your highness!

AUTHOR BIO

Nancy Blanton has worked as a journalist, magazine editor, corporate communications leader and brand manager. She has a bachelor's degree in journalism, a master's degree in mass communications, and has won numerous awards for professional leadership, writing, advertising and public relations products.

Her novel *Sharavogue* won first place for historical fiction in Florida's Royal Palm Literary Awards. She has more books in process. She wrote and illustrated a children's book, *The Curious Adventure of Roodle Jones*; co-authored the award-winning book *Heaven on the Half Shell: the Story of the Pacific Northwest's Love Affair with the Oyster*; and spearheaded production of *Rising Tides and Tailwinds*, a corporate history book for the Port of Seattle centennial.

Her blog, *My Lady's Closet*, focuses on writing, books, book promotion and historical fiction—with a bit of research and travel thrown in for good measure.

Nancy lives in Florida with her husband Karl, two Labrador retrievers and two cats.

Connect with Nancy:
Blog: nancyblanton.com
Facebook: Nancy Blanton.Author
Twitter: @nancy_blanton

IMAGE CREDITS

Cover: Her royal highness sitting on a throne. © NejroN Photo. Bigstockphoto.com

Page 1, King Henry VIIII of England
Hans Holbein the Younger [Public domain], Wikimedia Commons
http://commons.wikimedia.org/wiki/File%3AHans_Holbein%2C
_the_Younger%2C_Around_1497-1543_-
_Portrait_of_Henry_VIII_of_England__Google_Art_Project.jpg

Page 5, Hatshepsut
By Rob Koopman from Leiderdorp, Netherlands (Maat-ka-Re
Hatsjepsoet (RMO Leiden)) [CC BY-SA 2.0
(http://creativecommons.org/licenses/by-sa/2.0)], Wikimedia
Commons
http://commons.wikimedia.org/wiki/File%3AWLANL_-
koopmanrob-_Maat-ka-Re_Hatsjepsoet_(RMO_Leiden).jpg

Page 9, A portraiture of Henry VIII by the workshop of Hans
Holbein the Younger. This work is in the public domain in the
United States because it was published (or registered with the U.S.
Copyright Office) before January 1, 1923.
http://commons.wikimedia.org/wiki/File%3AWorkshop_of_Hans
_Holbein_the_Younger_-_Portrait_of_Henry_VIII_-
_Google_Art_Project.jpg

Page 13, Elizabeth I (Armada Portrait)
Formerly attributed to George Gower [Public domain], Wikimedia
Commons
https://commons.wikimedia.org/wiki/File%3AElizabeth_I_(Arma
da_Portrait)

Page 16, Queen Elizabeth, Rainbow Portrait
Attributed to Isaac Oliver [Public domain], Wikimedia Commons

http://commons.wikimedia.org/wiki/File%3AElizabeth_I_Rainbow_Portrait.jpg

Page 19, Louis XIV in Coronation Robes by Hyacinthe Rigaud (1701), Public Domain
http://commons.wikimedia.org/wiki/File:Louis_XIV_of_France.jpg

Page 21, Louis XIV Equestrian Portrait
Pierre Mignard [Public domain], Wikimedia Commons
http://commons.wikimedia.org/wiki/File%3AEquestrian_portrait_louis_xiv_1692.jpg

Page 23, Napoleon Crossing the Alps
Jérôme-Martin Langlois [Public domain], Wikimedia Commons
http://commons.wikimedia.org/wiki/File%3AJacques_Louis_David__Bonaparte_franchissant_le_Grand_Saint-Bernard%2C_20_mai_1800_-_Google_Art_Project.jpg

Page 25, Portrait of Napoleon Bonaparte
By Alexandre Benoit Jean Dufay [Public domain], Wikimedia Commons
http://commons.wikimedia.org/wiki/File%3AAlexandre_Benoit_Jean_Dufay%2C_Casanova_(Paris_17701844)%2C_Portrait_of_the_Emperor_Napoleon_Bonaparte.

Page 27, Lincoln portrait
George Peter Alexander Healy [Public domain], Wikimedia Commons
http://commons.wikimedia.org/wiki/File%3AAbrahamLincolnOilPainting1869Restored.jpg

Page 30, John F. Kennedy portrait
Aaron Shikler [Public domain], via Wikimedia Commons
http://commons.wikimedia.org/wiki/File%3AJohn_F_Kennedy_Official_Portrait.jpg

SELECTED SOURCES

Burke, Peter. The Fabrication of Louis XIV. Yale
University Press, New Haven and London, 1992.

Rapelli, Paola. Symbols of Power in Art. J. Paul Getty
Museum, Los Angeles, 2011.

NOTES